oyster culture

oyster culture

BY GWENDOLYN MEYER
& DOREEN SCHMID

 CAMERON + COMPANY

for D.J.Meyer

Copyright © 2011 Cameron + Company
Library of Congress Control Number: 2011927268
ISBN 9780918684875

Photography: Gwendolyn Meyer © 2011 Gwendolyn Meyer

design: vision road design, visionroaddesign.com
typography: the natural space, thenaturalspace.com

Images courtesy of:
pg 31, 32, 33, 34 courtesy of The Bancroft Library,
University of California, Berkeley
pg ii-iii, 28-29, 76 (photographer Ella Jorgensen) pg 77,
courtesy of Point Reyes National Seashore Museum
pg 35, 74 courtesy of the Tomales Region History Center
pg 1, 24, 25, 27 Archival Photographer Stefan Claesson,
Gulf of Maine Cod Project, NOAA National Marine Sanctuaries;
courtesy of National Archives, 1889
pg 29 courtesy of Anne Kent Room, Marin County Free Library
pg 101 courtesy of Dave Mitchell, Point Reyes Light, May 1980

Cameron + Company
6 Petaluma Boulevard North, Suite B6, Petaluma, CA 94952
www.cameronbooks.com
800.779.5582

Cameron + Company is a boutique publishing house, creating and
distributing quality books and calendars since 1964 with a focus on
photography, art, architecture, and publications of regional interest.

First Edition
10 9 8 7 6 5 4 3 2 1
Printed in Thailand

contents

DEPARTMENT OF COMMERCE
U. S. BUREAU OF FISHERIES
WASHINGTON

WHY YOU SHOULD EAT OYSTERS

The *Oyster Production* of the United States is the *Greatest in the World*.

It can be *Made Much Greater* because vast areas of unproductive bottom can be made productive *by Oyster Culture*.

The *Purity* of oysters placed on the market is now *More Assured by United States and State Inspection* and the cooperation of the large producers.

Don't be afraid of *Green Gilled Oysters*. The gray-green color, which is of vegetable origin and derived from their food, forms a deep fringe within the open edge of the oyster. Such oysters are *Often the Best* and in France are prized above all others.

Therefore Eat Oysters

It is *A Duty* to utilize this vast food resource as far as possible and save other foods of which there is a dearth.

It is also *A Pleasure* to use the oyster which in other countries than ours is a luxury rather than a common food.

It is not one of the cheap foods when measured by the cost of its useful constituents, but it is valuable as *an Appetizing Variant of the Diet*. A reasonable variety of food is necessary to the health of a civilized people.

The oyster is *Without Waste, Digestible, Wholesome, and Delicious*, and it may be *Prepared in Many Ways*. If you wish to know how, *Write for a Cook Book*, to—

U. S. BUREAU OF FISHERIES, DIVISION F,
WASHINGTON, D. C.

Introduction

Oysters are coveted and cultivated for many reasons: their taste, texture, and proverbial amatory reputation. We savor their salinity, a state that reflects our own corporeal composition. Add to their allure the fact that they sometimes harbor a hidden treasure—the pearl.

Oyster Culture is about the pleasures of oysters, as well as the way that they have shaped the social and physical landscape of coastal northern California, and particularly West Marin.

Food, farming, and conservation have deeply influenced the communities surrounding Tomales Bay and Drakes Estero. People, place, and politics here are entwined with oyster cultivation and consumption, pursuits and pleasures that have long been part of the larger Bay Area's cultural and culinary history. Early Native American Coastal Miwoks ate them, Gold Rush oyster stews were served to miners in the camps, and the crème de la crème of San Francisco society, and its robber barons, cultivated a voracious appetite for them. Today passionate locavores intent upon fresh, place-based foods award oysters a prime place in an evolving regional cuisine. The threats to successful continuity of oyster farming here and the protective measures governing agencies have instituted to help the industry survive are an integral part of this story.

Both sustenance and sustainability define oyster consumption through the ages. Wherever archaeological remains of coastal dweller meals are found, oyster shells are sure to be on the menu, going back to Neolithic times. What might seem luxurious (their diet also included lobster, then plentiful, and wild, now "exotic" game) was then just about what was available. Today, oyster eating can seem a luxury, or reflect sustainability, the ultimate privilege-informed diet.

In West Marin, oysters cross culinary lines—shucked and slurped seaside; served raw on ice and seaweed in white-tablecloth restaurants; and enjoyed at Mexican, Anglo and Asian barbeques, usually with spiced or hot sauces.

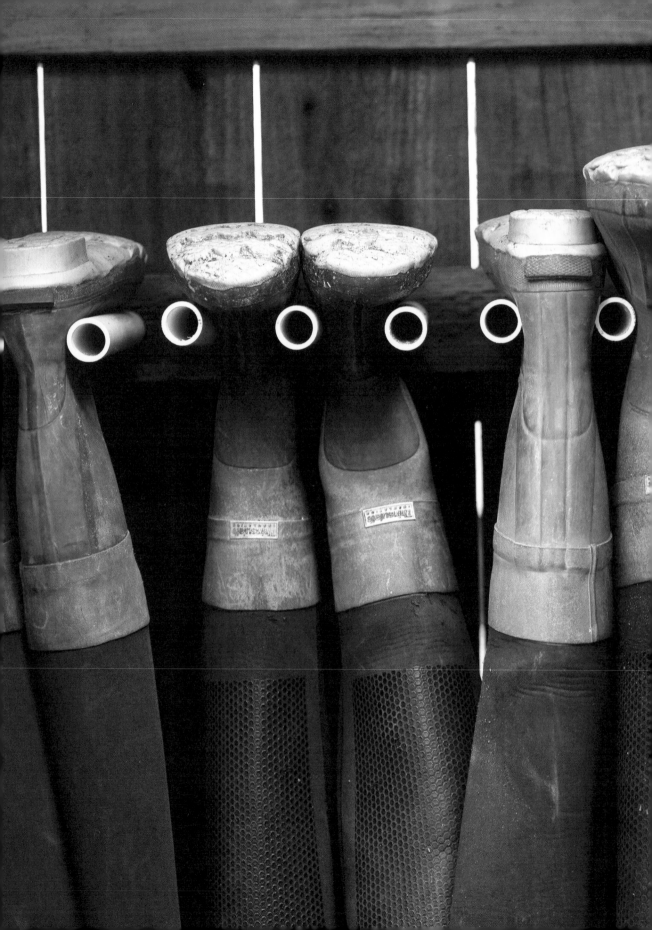

reconsidering the oyster

Sustenance and Symbiosis

Oysters result from a fortuitous culmination of circumstances. The combination of clean estuaries, good tidal flow, and nutrient-rich seasonal ocean upwelling produces an edible hard-shelled delicacy that is a renowned culinary triumph of flavor. Only such perfectly aligned conditions are likely to produce an oyster suitable for eating, whether wild or farmed. Unfortunately, today there are fewer places where these environments exist. Worldwide, clean estuaries and tidal zones are disappearing or are impacted by increasing coastal populations and the rising risk of manmade environmental disasters such as oil spills that destroy habitats and pollute sensitive tidal zones.

An hour north of the San Francisco Bay, the long narrow Tomales Bay and the Drakes Estero are two unique habitats that have supported a rich aquaculture industry for over a century. These two bodies of water remain relatively pristine, surrounded by protected pubic land and agricultural land trusts. Here in this foggy landscape, oyster farmers contend with the caprices of nature and the occasional difficulties arising from working in a commercial industry in or surrounded by public, federally protected lands.

"Place-based food" possesses a healthy symbiotic relationship with its environment, including cultural associations with its producer. In a time of global warming, climate change, and the increasing expense of extracting fossil fuels, local, sustainably produced foods help the environment, support farmer to community relationships, and promote cultural and regional typicity.

Since the 1950s the demand for fish has shot up so rapidly that supply has plummeted drastically. Fishery management has improved significantly and slowly supplies are once again growing, but not significantly enough to meet the continually growing demand. The U.S. imports 87% of its seafood and it is estimated that in ten years an additional 1.1 million metric tons will be required to meet demand—a staggering increase that wild fisheries just cannot supply. In the next decade most seafood we eat will be farm raised. But farm-raised fish can harm the environment as well as human health. Oyster farms stand out as sustainability models for farmed seafood: they benefit the environment while producing a prized food source. Oyster farming's environmental footprint is minimal, requiring very little fresh water, no fertilizer or pesticides. Almost by default, oysters farmers are environmental stewards—because bivalves possess built-in ecological benefits.

Beneficial Bivalves

Although oysters have been enjoyed as a culinary delicacy since Roman times, it is only recently that their environmental advantages have been recognized. Think of oysters as prognosticators of pollution and oyster reefs as ecosystem engineers: if you can safely eat an oyster it means it comes from a clean estuarine system.

Healthy oyster reefs are a proven way to effectively reduce water pollution and improve the marine environment. While other bivalves also possess the ingenious ability to clean water through flushing out pollutants as they feed, none are simultaneous symbols of feasting, as is the oyster. As an oyster filters water through its body (up to 5 liters of water an hour), it siphons out and discards pollutants such as nitrogen. A lack of oxygen is detrimental to all species, yet in excess nitrogen causes environmental harm, depleting oxygen and causing algal blooms that make water turbid or cloudy. Found in fertilizer and sewage, it is the main culprit behind the spoilage of two thirds of U.S. waterways. Oyster aquaculture acts as a watchdog of waterways, as shellfish cultivation requires extremely high water quality standards and the slightest rise in pollutant runoff can result in the closure of strictly monitored farms.

Oyster reefs are complex shell cluster structures that build up over time. Both these naturally occurring reefs and oyster cultivation, which involves bags and hanging cultures, provide a hospitable habitat for eelgrass, crabs, and fish. The native Olympia reefs that are being reintroduced into San Francisco Bay are attracting increasingly diverse fish populations, including the juvenile Chinook salmon and the endangered Bay Gobi. Invertebrates such as clams and worms feed off the detritus surrounding the reefs or oyster gardens, and add to the thick layers. A reef's solid structure also slows shoreline erosion.

According to the Nature Conservancy, 85% of natural reefs worldwide have disappeared, making them one of the world's most severely impacted marine environments. In the 1700s the oyster reefs on Virginia's Chesapeake Bay were so large that they were mapped as a navigational hazard. Today those reefs are reduced to 1% of their earlier size, and the Bay is severely polluted. Previously the reefs kept the water pure by acting as a massive filtration system, cleaning out its eighteen trillion gallons of water every three to four days. Chesapeake Bay is one of many places where oysters are being reintroduced in an effort to improve water quality.

Reintroducing the Native

Oyster reefs and other helpful environments such as eelgrass beds are considered keystone species, meaning habitats that benefit other species. The National Oceanic and Atmospheric Administration (NOAA) has a mandate to restore these environments throughout the U.S., as they provide havens for diverse fish species. Until the 1990s, Olympia oysters were found in San Francisco Bay, surprisingly in some of its most polluted waters near the Chevron Refinery in Richmond. But by 2001 the Bay's Olympia oysters were thought extinct. "We know how to destroy but don't know how to make habitat," marine biologist Robert Abbott says. Today reclamation projects such as his Wild Oyster Restoration are building starter habitats in the Bay. Local restoration volunteer initiatives for the Olympia oyster include Hog Island Oyster Company's experimental Olympia farming for purposes of both habitat restoration and consumption. Drakes Bay Oyster Company donates shells that are used in habitat restoration projects.

Within a short time hundreds of thousands of native, wild Olympia oysters will populate the false reefs in San Francisco Bay. Once they are established, thousands of smelt, green sturgeon, perch and pipefish will use the habitat as a feeding ground. Another issue Abbott raises is "the question of how to establish a hard structure in the water column that does not disappear into the mud." Mud and sediment in the Bay can suffocate and smother the colonies; however once a set of oysters is established, they grow vertically and can survive sediment.

"We know how to destroy but don't know how to make habitat"

OYSTERS LIVE IN estua-
rine systems, and cannot survive
without salty water, even if brack-
ish. The taste of an oyster differs
throughout the year, influenced
by seasonal flows of fresh or salty
water: the saltier the water the
brinier the oyster. The Tomales
Bay's delicately balanced estuarine
ecosystem provides a unique and
relatively pristine habitat for wild
and farmed oysters.

Study of an Ecosystem

An estuary is where the river meets the ocean. The Tomales Bay is an estuary, a habitat where salt water and fresh water mix. Estuaries are dynamic and valuable ecosystems, each with their own unique biodiversity. Healthy estuaries act as transition zones between the ocean and land; their calm and protective waters provide habitats for a diversity of species, specially adapted to the dynamic environment where tides and rains change conditions on a daily and seasonal basis. Because of their protected, shallow habitats, estuaries are ideal nurseries for juvenile fish and invertebrates, safe from many larger predators roaming the sea. In California, estuaries and wetlands have been heavily impacted by human activity and invasion by non-native species. Development, sedimentation, and contaminant runoff have resulted in a substantial loss of habitat and declines in ecosystems' natural function. Although considered "impaired," the Tomales Bay is one of the last relatively pristine estuarine ecosystems left in California. As Lagunitas Creek in the south and Walker Creek to the north feed into the Tomales Bay, they travel through ranchlands, many of which have adopted protective measures limiting pollution that can compromise the health of these waters. Limited development and an active conservation-minded community in the Tomales Bay watershed have helped to protect the health of this estuarine environment.

Seasonally hypersaline, the bay is landlocked on three sides and becomes saltier and warmer than the ocean in the summer dry season. Strong tidal flows in the outer bay, near the narrow mouth, north of Hog Island, bring in salty and cold ocean water, while the strong sun warms and evaporates water in the shallows toward the upper bay. Seasons influence the bay: offshore upwelling of deep ocean water from spring through summer brings colder and nutrient-rich water into the bay. As winter progresses, rains bring fresh water runoff from rivers and groundwater seeps, carrying an abundance of nutrients from upland surfaces. These seasonal cycles create a vital, productive, and nutrient-rich system that feeds all life in the bay.

This long and narrow bay lies over California's most famous fault, the mile-and-a-half wide San Andreas, which runs in a straight line deep below it. Rolling hills and grasslands cover the sandy loam soils of the continental shelf on the eastern shore. Bishop Pine, Oak, Bay and Madrone forests are on the granitic western shore.

a taste for the bivalve

West Coast Wild

There is a popular myth that Easterners' appetites wiped out the native San Francisco oyster by over-harvesting it, yet despite these accounts, it appears that the newly arrived immigrants did not have much of an appetite for the native California oyster. The flavor of the small local Olympia was described as "coppery" and inferior to Eastern or Atlantic oysters. It was cursed as a "bastard oyster" by early local oystermen, probably out of frustration at the size and flavor, and the inability to find a suitable native crop to satisfy the huge demand for oysters.

In his 1892 book *Chronicles of the Builders of the Commonwealth*, Hubert Howe Bancroft reveals local sentiment towards the lowly local Olympia. He epitomizes an oysterman's disgust at a product that cannot satisfy his customers: "Perhaps there is not one person in a hundred in this state who realizes that there is actually no such thing as a California oyster. The only California product of the kind that bears any resemblance to an oyster is a little soft-shelled parasite, more like a barnacle … a handful of which can be squeezed up into a pulp with slight pressure. They are not fit for consumption."

Bancroft describes the lack of a sufficient local supply. His biography on John Morgan, founder of one of San Francisco's first oyster companies, the Morgan Oyster Company, recounts how early entrepreneurial San Francisco oyster companies investigated possible production areas of wild oyster seed up and down the West Coast including West Marin. Their search for a large and abundant source of wild oyster seed close to the San Francisco market was without much luck. Some native oysters were harvested from Tomales Bay before 1870 for the San Francisco market, but most came from Washington's Shoalwater Bay (now known as Willapa Bay).

Archeological evidence that presents us with proof that the local Olympia oyster was once present in great numbers in San Francisco Bay, also shows a gradual decline in numbers by the time of the arrival of Europeans, possibly because of environmental changes. The study of shell middens, the material records of the diets of Coast Miwok Indians, reveals higher concentrations of mussel and clamshells in the top layers, with oyster shells present in the bottom layers, indicating that in more recent historical times, wild oysters had become less prominent in their diet.

CALIFORNIA'S NATIVE OLYMPIA oyster, the Ostreo Lurida, is found along the Pacific coast from Alaska to Baja California. Size varies by location; those found in the Bay area are smaller in size than their Washington counterparts.

Culling Oysters; Single float
in background; Scows etc.
Company St

165.

The Bay Oyster Society

Packing Boxes. San Francisco

Short-lived, yet booming while it lasted, San Francisco's oyster industry started during the Gold Rush Days in response to the appetites of newly arrived East Coast immigrants, who had a taste for cheap, plentiful oysters. The industry relied upon imports: first from Washington, and later from the Atlantic coast. The San Francisco Bay eventually became too polluted and silted in to support oyster farming. The oyster industry would probably never have arrived in Tomales Bay had San Francisco's oyster farms continued to thrive. San Franciscans had a big taste for the bivalve.

San Francisco oyster wholesalers began by buying mature Olympias, or "Olys" from Washington's Willapa Bay Native Americans. They supplied the early San Francisco industry for almost forty years despite what in those days was the great distance of seven hundred miles. Holding pens to refresh oysters after their long journey lined the western and southern shores of the San Francisco Bay.

Oyster companies turned to importing the East Coast or Atlantic oyster in 1869, when the First Transcontinental Railroad was completed. The Atlantics, preferred both in flavor and size, arrived by the trainload. Mature Atlantics were "fattened" in the shallow tidelands for about a month and then sold. But transporting mature oysters was costly and companies soon turned to importing seed, frozen in barrels of water. The seed was broadcast on old broken oyster shells to set in "cultches," probably based on the French method of oyster farming. Spat attached to the old shells and formed clusters, maturing into oysters that were collected by raking.

San Francisco's oyster beds then were prized. As proclaimed in 1909 in the daily *San Francisco Call*: "It would take the pen of a poet guided by the imagination of an epicure to do any sort of justice to the oysters of San Francisco. The oyster of San Francisco is famous. Its celebrity has gone forth to the ends of the earth, carried by the eloquent tongues of the gourmand, native or visitor, who has tasted, smacked his lips, tasted again, and instantly has become the willing slave to the appetite for the delicious bivalve that thrives upon the oyster beds of San Francisco Bay."

A growing immigrant population not only created the market, but also contributed to its decline. This population spurt caused pollution in the Bay, a problem compounded by sediment and mud runoff from gold mining in the Sierras that smothered the oyster beds. The San Francisco industry began to collapse at around the same time *The Call* sang its praises. As the Bay became increasingly polluted, companies looked for new tidal lands to farm. Tomales Bay's cleaner water offered promise as a new supply grounds, and the newly completed North Pacific Coast Railroad provided transport from West Marin farms to the city. By 1939, when the last oysters were commercially harvested in San Francisco, Tomales Bay oyster companies were in full swing.

"It would take the pen of a poet guided by the imagination of an epicure to do any sort of justice to the oysters of San Francisco."

Oyster bed fence.
San Francisco Bay.
Cal.
About 1889

FENCES SURROUNDING
THE beds kept out bat rays,
which farmers believed were the
worst of oyster predators, next to
the notorious San Francisco "oyster pirates," who poached and sold
oysters in the Oakland markets.

North Pacific Coast Railroad.

202	Not good unless dated on the back.	SAUCELITO —TO— TOMALES.
	Whole.	*G. F. Harlwil* Superintendent.

Issued by North Pacific Coast Railroad.

202	Not good unless dated on the back.	Saucelito Ferry.	
		27 Whole.	SAN FRANCISCO —TO— SAUCELITO.

THE TOMALES BAY region was too remote to be a real supply option until the North Pacific Coast Railroad made transport of perishables a reality, leading to the development of oyster farms and other businesses.

THE NORTH PACIFIC Coast Railroad that ran along the Tomales Bay's east shore was built to connect the Redwood Empire in the north with Sausalito and, with a ferry ride at the end, San Francisco in the south. The track ran from eastern Marin across what is now Samuel P. Taylor State Park, switched to a narrow gauge at "the barn" (once red, now green), a Point Reyes landmark, and headed north to Cazadero, gateway to the Redwood Empire.

FROM 1875 TO the 1930s, fisheries, canning companies and oyster farms sprang up along Tomales Bay's east shore, making it a busy and successful commercial food-producing hub. The train connected the towns of Marshall, Tomales and Dillon Beach to points north and south. Stations included Bivalve, Millerton, Fisherman's, Marshall and Hamlet. The train also became a popular recreational passenger route, bringing early tourists to the area.

Even before the train provided transport, West Marin had established a reputation for producing and shipping fine food products. Its prized commodities included butter from the Pierce Point dairies, hogs, beef, and potatoes, all shipped to market on schooners stopping at various shipping points along the Bay, including Keys Creek and Pierce Point. Transporting fresh goods by road was not a viable option in the late 1800s, and with cars another quarter century off, existing road transportation was slow, and in bad weather often impossible. Fortunately the Bay was still deep enough for vessels to navigate, both for exporting food and for importing supplies for local farms. But the success and expansion of agriculture in West Marin led to permanent and irreversible changes to the Bay.

Between 1852 and 1902 an average of two thousand tons of soil per square mile washed into Keys Creek. This rapid erosion from farming and forestry eventually eliminated water traffic. Upriver shipping warehouses were forced to move downstream. By 1918 the marsh at the Bay's southern end had migrated one kilometer towards the ocean and vessels were no longer able to reach Lagunitas Creek. The siltation problem persisted through the nineteenth century and continues today, making the southern part of the Bay at its deepest no more than nine feet. Millerton Point tidal flats had three to five feet of water at high tide in the 1920s and by the 1960s never more than a foot. Without the new railroad making transport possible the oyster farming industry wouldn't have survived. As the inevitable decline of production in San Francisco became apparent oyster companies increasingly looked to Tomales Bay's pristine estuary system as the next best option: a market close enough to the city and with modern transport.

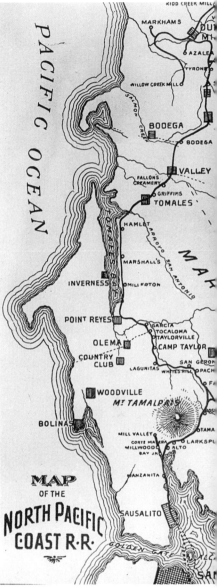

Eastern oysters were first planted in Tomales Bay in 1874, the same year the railroad track was completed. There is not much known about who started the area's first oyster plantings at Millerton Point, except that their venture was not long lived, possibly because the San Francisco industry was still thriving. In the early 1900s, when it became crucial to identify new growing grounds, San Francisco oyster companies started moving into Tomales Bay. The Pacific Coast Oyster Company began operating in Bivalve in 1907, at the Bay's south end, using its own private company train station. Gilbert Oyster Company followed with plantings near Millerton Point in 1909. In 1913 Tomales Bay Oyster Company was started. Initial plantings were of Atlantic oysters, using the San Francisco cultch growing method. By 1919 Tomales Bay was growing 24% of California's oysters.

Farming was more luck than science in the early days; seed was broad-casted onto the mud flats at low tide. Harvesting was equally straightforward: a farmer walked out onto the flats at low tide and picked up the mature oysters. Yields were irregular, as stormy weather could wash away oysters or runoff could completely cover their beds in mud. Farms that lost their oyster beds to mud and their tidal zones to siltation were frequently forced to merge or close. Today there are five oyster operations on Tomales Bay. Vestiges of early oyster farms are still visible at low tide at Bivalve and Millerton. The Tomales Bay Oyster Company is the only original farm left on the Bay.

As tourism has grown the oyster industry has benefited—each successive generation brought a new wave of oyster lovers to the Bay for the scenery and the oysters grown just feet away from where they are enjoyed. Oyster and dairy farms and restaurants produce and serve up regional food and continue to make the Tomales Bay an area rich in history and scenic agricultural vistas, and home to people whose livelihood and pleasures are part of the place where they live.

The Mighty Pacific Oyster

Although the railroad supported the oyster industry's growth by providing relatively quick transport of fresh oysters to the city's markets, the introduction of the Pacific Oyster radically changed West Coast oyster farming. In the 1920s the Department of Fish and Game began research on expanding and promoting the California oyster industry on a large scale. Their goal was to limit invasive species and import a cost-effective seed. Eastern oysters had been grown in Tomales Bay, but this practice had also introduced a deadly oyster predator, the Atlantic drill, to both the Tomales and San Francisco Bays, the latter being one of the most invaded estuaries in the world.

The Department of Fish and Game considered Morro Bay, Tomales Bay and Drakes Estero suitable sites for experimenting and for expanding the industry, although Tomales Bay wasn't a candidate for large-scale expansion because of its limited tidal flats. Despite this, the Department of Fish and Game began the first experimental planting of the Japanese Pacific Oyster, in partnership with Tomales Bay Oyster Company, in 1928. Crassostrea gigas, the giant cupped, Japanese or Miyagi oyster, possessed great market potential, and it was cheaper to import the seed from Japan than from the East Coast. The first harvest in 1935 definitively proved that Tomales Bay could produce an exceptional Pacific oyster from Japanese seed.

For a brief moment in the 1950s Tomales Bay was the largest oyster producer in California. Today it is the state's smallest production area, but home of its oldest oyster farm and last oyster-canning factory, at Drakes Bay Estero.

JAPANESE SEED OYSTERS come from Matsushima Bay in Miyagi Prefecture, about 250 miles north of Tokyo, where they have been growing seed oysters for later transplant for over 300 years. The oyster shells with spat sets are carefully prepared for shipment by incremental removal from the tidal zone, then packed in seaweed and shipped across the ocean.

THE WEST COAST, including California, became a huge market for importing Japanese seed. Oyster farmers bought their seed from Japanese farm representatives until the Pacific Coast Oyster Growers Association was founded to broker sales. During World War II transport was interrupted and seed buying slowed. After the war many farmers preferred to make their own buying trips to Japan.

MORE RECENTLY THE Kumamoto Prefecture has become a source of seed for export to the United States. The Pacific or Miyagi oysters produced in Kumamoto Prefecture are smaller and rounder, with a deep cup, and are regarded as superior in shape and taste, although slower growing and therefore less profitable than the larger Miyagi oysters.

aquaculture

Oyster Companies

Oysters are California's oldest aquaculture industry. The development of innovative farming techniques such as the "cultch less" method have allowed the industry to survive as well as flourish. With its irregular shoreline, the narrow Tomales Bay has limited tidal flats suitable for oyster cultivation. But its relatively calm waters, gentle tides, and sandy mud bottom are suited to growing oyster singles in bottom bags or bags suspended on racks.

The California Department of Fish and Game leases about 5% of Tomales Bay's water acreage to five aquaculture companies, all located on Marin's eastern shore. The leases range in size from 5 to 150 acres. Hog Island Oyster Company and Tomales Bay Oyster Company, the largest ones, run waterside retail sales operations alongside picnic areas for customers, as well as sell wholesale to restaurants and seafood brokers. They farm between Hog Island and Preston Point at the mouth of Walker Creek on tidal flats that enjoy good water flow and "water time" or the time the developing oysters spend submerged in water.

The three other brands—Point Reyes Oyster Company, Cove Mussel Company, and the Marin Oyster Company—are smaller, and mostly whole-sale. Sales of oysters, mussels, and clams account for millions of dollars in sales in Marin County yearly, and provide a livelihood for many people. Growing methods have evolved over the years, but a farmer's dependence on tides and water quality remains a constant, as does patience, since oysters can take up to two years to mature.

Each company on Tomales Bay has its own approach to oyster farming. Growing methods are customized to tidal flow, management and removal of predators, and optimizing the shape and depth of the oyster shell. Different farming methods produce a slightly different product and producers are known for their product profiles, distinctive in shape and flavor, akin to a winery's "house style." Hog Island uses a rack and bag method to keep its oysters above the mud, resulting in a "sweet water" taste. Tomales Bay Oyster Company toughens its oyster shells, hardening them by flipping and stressing the shell, which encourages the growth of their signature sweet plump oyster housed in a deep protective shell.

Tomales Bay Oyster Co.

Tomales Bay Oyster Company is the longest continually operating oyster farm in California. Originally called Morgan's Tomales Bay Fishery, it became Tomales Bay Oyster Company in 1913. Oscar Johannson farmed for the company for sixty-two years. It was sold in 1988 to Drew Alden. Alden initially supplied a busy retail market with oysters from Tomales Bay. As demand grew he began selling oysters from the Morro Bay farm he owned in the San Luis Obispo area, and also imported Washington oysters.

Tod Friend, a former Hog Island Oyster Company farmer and retail manager, bought Tomales Bay Oyster Company in 2009. He shares ownership with daughter Heidi Gregory and son Shannon, who also, along with Kim Labao, own and operate The Marshall Store. Friend farms medium, small, and extra small oysters on his leases on the prime tidal flats at Preston Point. Mussels and tumbled oysters known as nuggets are farmed at Tomasini Point, close to the retail site. Tomales Bay Oyster Company retail sales are as high as three million oysters a year, mostly grown in Tomales Bay. A lively and popular weekend destination, people barbeque and picnic here along the waterfront, enjoying "farm fresh" oysters, mussels and clams.

Producers are known for their product profiles, distinct in shape and flavor, akin to a winery's "house style."

Hog Island Oyster Co.

The philosophy behind the Hog Island Oyster Company is simple: produce a high-quality oyster, develop high brand visibility and keep a close eye on quality maintenance. Their philosophy is also deeply rooted in stewardship of the environment in which they farm. Hog Island directly distributes to its wholesale customers to ensure that a quality product arrives at their door. Because Tomales Bay is part of the Gulf of the Farallones National Marine Sanctuary, the farm, like all those within this sanctuary, works with over twenty agencies that manage land use and water quality in and around the Bay.

Hog Island Oyster Company is currently in the certification process to become the nation's first shellfish farm recognized for upholding food quality, stewardship of the land and minimizing harmful downstream impacts. The company's owners recognize that their farm provides an economic and cultural benefit to the community in a unique area and ecosystem. As co-owner Terry Sawyer says, "None of this would be here without the Point Reyes National Seashore—we all owe a huge debt to its creation." The farm produces small to medium Pacific oysters, Kumomoto oysters, clams and is experimenting with growing Washington "Olys." They also have a popular shoreside barbeque and picnic area for customers.

"None of this would be here without the Point Reyes National Seashore—we all owe a huge debt to its creation."

The Community's Farm

Pickleweed Point is Tomales Bay's first community oyster farm. It is a natural fit for an area known for its emphasis on community, organic food, and collaborative efforts. The farm is modeled after examples in the Pacific Northwest. Members pay on a quantity basis, and the farm supplies each one with between two hundred and one thousand seeds. Members must complete a basic orientation on aquaculture and the Bay's ecology and are not allowed to commercially sell their oysters. A first-timer's initial planting is supervised and the farm allows members access at low tide for maintenance of the bags.

FOR MANY YEARS Drakes
Estero has been a well-known oyster location to visitors as well as
San Francisco restaurants. Its fin-
ger-shaped inlets provide an ideal,
sheltered environment for oyster
farming and are considered one of
California's most pristine bodies
of water. The 1,000-acre oyster
farming lease here spreads out over
the Estero and into Barries Bay,
Creamery Bay, Schooner Bay and
Home Bay.

Drakes Bay Oyster Co.

Pacific oysters were introduced in Drakes Estero in the 1930s, at about the same time experimental plantings began in Tomales Bay. Drakes Bay Oyster Company was established in 1935 and three years later the company started canning oysters for export. The lease area was legally reduced by two thirds in the 1950s and the balance designated as a clam and eelgrass preserve. Charlie Johnson started Johnson's Oyster Farm (now called Drakes Bay Family Farms, owners of Drakes Bay Oyster Company) in 1957. The Lunny family acquired Johnson's lease in 2004. A long-time farming family in the Point Reyes National Seashore (PRNS), the Lunnys also run the neighboring Historic G Ranch farm and have been farming cattle for eighty years. Drakes Estero produces an oyster that is distinct in taste—brinier, and saltier—from those found in Tomales Bay.

Kevin Lunny and his family face the unique challenge of trying to gain a special use permit to continue farming oysters in an area designated for national wilderness. The issue has become a nationally publicized battle and has two distinct sides: those who favor returning the area to wilderness and those who campaign for regional food sources and the positive effects of oyster farming. When PRNS was established, farms that existed within the proposed protected area were offered twenty, thirty and forty-year "reservation or right of use" (ROU) permits that allowed them to continue to farm for a certain period of time. Once the ROU expired, the farm would then be eligible for a subsequent special operation use permit at the discretion of the National Parks Service (NPS). Most farms opted back then for a twenty-year ROU. Charlie Johnson chose a forty-year one that expires in 2012.

EVERY OYSTER FARMER
must work closely with the
timing of the tides. Harvesting is
best performed at mid-tide, when
a boat can closely approach the
rows of bags. Low tides occur
during the day most of the year
except in November and late
December when the best tides
for harvesting occur in the late
afternoon. These are also the
months of big demand for oysters,
so harvesting often continues
well past dusk into the night.

Growing Oysters

All commercial oysters grown in the West Marin region start their
lives in a laboratory because of the Bay water's colder temperatures. The water
is too cold for either Pacific or Atlantic oysters to fertilize, although adults
do spawn in the summer months. Spawning oysters are edible but have a
milkier consistency.

An oyster starts its life as a planktonic larva, microscopic in size, and in an
average batch of a million eggs per spawn. Its sex will eventually be determined
by the water's salt content and temperature. As a miniscule swimming larva,
it consists of a tiny shell, muscle, and foot. The larva feeds on algae and after
ten to fifteen days, its swimming stage is over and it extends its foot, settles on
any solid object it can find no matter how small, and cements itself into place.
Now it is known as an oyster spat. The spat then grows into a seed oyster with
a protective shell.

Chris Starbird of Marshall supplies seed oysters for Tomales Bay Oyster Company and Hog Island. He uses a floating upwelling system, also known as a flupsy, to stimulate growth. The spat come from Washington, Humboldt Bay, Oregon or Hawaii. His flupsy system's pump and rudder pulls water up from the Bay and into bins containing the spat. This accelerated rate of water flow simulates the ocean's natural upwelling and causes oyster spat to grow quickly, fed and fluidized with Bay water rich in phytoplankton and zooplankton. The flupsy is strategically located to take advantage of the Bay's natural nutrient collection point. Once the oyster spat or seed oyster is large enough it is put out in mesh bags to mature in the Bay.

Hog Island uses Stanways, another method of placing spat out to grow. Stanways are floating cylinders, able to turn with the tide. They rotate on racks, stimulating growth and keeping the seed oysters moving and tumbling.

THE DRAKES BAY Oyster Company raises seed larvae in their own on-site laboratory. The larvae are so small that they can only be seen in quantities of thousands. They start out in water with a fine sand substrate; when the larvae reach the spat stage they are ready to be introduced to a permanent surface of discarded shells with holes drilled through them. This is done in the controlled environment of large circular vats with temperature-controlled water, sometimes referred to by company personnel as "oyster hot tubs." The water is kept warm to ensure the larvae's survival. Estero water is fed into the vats through a fine mesh so that particles larger than the spat will not enter. Once the spat is permanently fixed to the shells, the shells are strung on wire with spacers in a stringing shed and taken out to a rack in the Bay.

The larvae are so small that they can only be seen in quantities of thousands.

The larger the seed put out in bags, the faster it will grow, and the better chance it has of survival. Tomales Bay Oyster Company takes six-month-old seed out to the Tom's Point beds. The bags contain an average of 180 seeds each and are tied down by rope strung between rows of poles. At low tide a field of bags stretches into the distance, a row crop of oysters. At high tide, dozens of white PVC poles stick out of the water, marking the lease area.

The hanging cultch method, based on the hanging racks used in Japan, is the one most commonly used by Drakes Bay Oyster Company, and was adopted by Johnson (the earlier Johnson's Oyster Farm founder). Drakes is also experimenting with a French system of bottom bags and hanging pole cultures, which allows the oysters full access to the water column and its nutrients and keeps them above predators at the bottom. This may be the largest number of suspended wood platforms or bents in the U.S., all dating back to Johnson's time. The hanging farming method produces oyster cultches, the tight formations hardening and protecting the meat so that the end product is a well-protected, meaty oyster. This is a very labor-intensive method requiring multiple steps.

Some farmers harvest marketable product after a year; others wait a few years to let the shell deepen and harden in the first year and the meat to plump out in its second year. A crucial part of bottom bag growing is "flipping" bags back and forth with a hay hook, which helps harden the oyster shells, protecting the soft inside meat. This loosens predators that are boring through shells and prevents clustering. Flipping fifteen to twenty times a year also ensures a uniform size. A bag of oysters is very sturdy, and can support an average person's full weight without shattering; rather, the breaking and chipping of the shell edges actually strengthen the shell and toughen it up, further protecting the oyster meat inside.

Tomales Bay Oyster Company farmer Tod Friend describes his approach to growing: "I am exclusively a bottom bag farmer and so I have to flip the bags a lot to get a hard shell (strong bill), good shape (deep cup), and prevent 'clustering.' We are looking for nice singles, not doubles, or what are called clusters, and flipping the bags when we can get to them on the low tides helps produce the best results."

The rack and bag method used by Hog Island suspends bags above the mud. Instead of flipping, they "tip" the racks, using sticks or clubs to loosen the oysters that have been pushed into the corners by waves and wind.

Once harvested bottom bags are taken to shore, they are sprayed clean, sorted, and bagged for market. The bags are held in filtered and chilled Bay water in tanks for several days to clean the oyster of any mud inside and out. This tank cleaning is an important part of bottom bag farming as it eliminates grit. At Drakes the clusters are broken apart and intact single oysters are sold in the shell; those that are in tight clusters are schucked and jarred.

The water quality of Tomales Bay is closely monitored by more than a dozen agencies, and oyster companies play an important role in collecting data for them. On the first Tuesday of every month, the companies submit laboratory water test results to the California Department of Health Shellfish Monitoring Program. In winter, heavy rains can cause bacteria counts to rise in the Bay. Half an inch of rain causes immediate closure of harvesting for five days, and more rain extends the closure.

Drakes Estero is located in a much smaller watershed than Tomales Bay with less fresh water runoff, and the daily tidal flow flushes the Estero clean. Because of this, Estero oyster beds are less susceptible to rain closures.

EARLY OYSTER FARMERS built fences to protect their beds from the bat ray, often thought the oyster's worst enemy. Others believe, however, that crabs—both the native red rock crab and the imported European green one—are more voracious and predatory. Fences inadvertently did the early farmer a disservice by keeping out the ray, a crab predator. The main predators in the Tomales Bay are the Atlantic drill and red rock crabs. The Bay has varying levels of salinity and temperature. Atlantic drills are more prolific in the warmer water of the south Bay, and crabs favor the saltier, colder water near Tom's Point. Crabs hatch in the bags and become trapped there with a ready supply of food. A crab can work through an entire bag of oysters, using its pincers to open the shells and devour the meat inside.

Herring, and a Small Hamlet

With the advent of the railroad, Tomales Bay started to develop a thriving fishing industry supplying San Francisco's markets. The Bay's herring fishery attracted out-of-town commercial fisherman, and the Marshall Boat Works harbored many of their boats. The Bay's shallow, protected waters provided the perfect habitat for herring to spawn, and Tomales Bay herring was prized for their large size, and considered particularly good smoked or salted. There was a herring cannery in Hamlet, and the original Nick's Cove Restaurant smoked herring, as did the Consolidated Fisheries Company at Blake's Landing.

Until quite recently Japan was a huge market for California herring roe or Kazunoko, with a ton of herring fetching between $2,500 and $3,000. But demand led to decline, and by the 1970s overfishing caused the industry to fail. The Department of Fish and Game introduced strict catch-quotas to protect herring, with Tomales Bay's quotas regulated even more stringently than San Francisco's. By 1989 the average yield had dropped to forty tons, down from an average of five hundred and fifty tons a few years earlier. Fishermen, and their buyers and shippers, have disappeared from the once-busy center of this local industry. Marshall now has only one operational herring boat.

The small settlement of Hamlet, opposite Preston Point and close to Walker Creek's mouth, was one of the Bay's earliest oyster farms. Miwok Indians called it "Shatomko" and used its naturally protected location for thousands of years as a gathering place. Folklore has it that the Indians gathered there to see the white sails of the Spanish ships coming into the Bay. Since approximately 1917 it was an oyster lease, run by the Jensen family, and a whistle-stop on the early railroad route; it also had its own post office. Henry Jensen, Sr., sold herring and oysters for a dollar per sack. Jensen's son, Henry Jensen, Jr., and his Miwok wife Virginia inherited the farm in 1955 and experimented with various types of oysters and growing methods. Over the years, Jensen's Oyster Beds and Restaurant grew into a popular and well-known

Hamlet Cal

roadside attraction. Serving a full menu of oysters—barbequed, steamed, baked or on the half shell and in a renowned chowder—its catchy tagline "the oysters you buy today, slept in Tomales Bay last night" was a great customer draw. In 1987 the land was sold to the Golden Gate Recreational Area after years of struggle to maintain the business. The buildings on the property were abandoned, fell into disrepair, and were removed by the National Park Service in 2003. Many area residents objected to the removal of Hamlet's vernacular architecture. The loss of the site's potential to preserve cultural history represents a contentious issue and an ongoing struggle between the NPS's mandate to protect and preserve the wild, and the community's desire to preserve local cultural heritage and the human contribution to a place. Still occasionally identified on maps, today the town is an empty lot bearing no trace of the past.

Few remnants of most early Tomales Bay Area industries remain today. A visitor to the Bay can easily believe the area always appeared as it does now, scenic recreational land with little trace of human activity. Nothing much is left of the North Pacific Coast Railroad, which was deconstructed in the late 1930s to make way for improved roads and increasingly popular car travel. Its tracks were torn out in the 1940s and the steel donated to the WWII effort; all that is left are a few pieces of wood scattered along the old route and the berms that once enabled the train to cross tidal areas.

In the early 1970s, as the county planned to bring millions of visitors to the newly created PRNS, the idea of bringing back the train surfaced briefly as a way to reduce car travel. In his "To the Point" article in a 1971 issue of the local *Point Reyes Light*, editor Mike Gahagan agrees with the anti-car advocates who suggested the railroad as a solution: "Nowadays those that are against something usually have thought of an excellent alternative. If you want to ban the car, nix a national parkway [highway], then you better have something good up your sleeve ... You know what some of these anti-car people said? Bring the train back ... it worked before. It was a great way to travel. It was fun. It was exciting. It was safe. Why can't it work again? And you ask yourself, why can't it?"

"Bring the train back ... it worked before. It was a great way to travel. It was fun. It was exciting. It was safe. Why can't it work again? And you ask yourself, why can't it?"

the world loves oysters

"As I ate the oysters with their strong taste of the sea and their faint metallic taste that the cold white wine washed away, leaving only the sea taste and the succulent texture, and as I drank their cold liquid from each shell and washed it down with the crisp taste of the wine, I lost the empty feeling and began to be happy and to make plans."

— Ernest Hemingway, *A Moveable Feast*

How to Eat an Oyster

… with reverence. Like a child listening for the sea in a shell, eating a fresh oyster is like tasting the entire ocean. It is a fundamental flavor experience, like eating truffles or drinking a fine regional wine.

The hard shell in your hand is crusty, ridged and brown. It is closed, seemingly sealed and inaccessible. The knife targets the hidden joint and, with a flick of the wrist, you disconnect the top shell from the bottom. Discard the covering, then the bottom bowl, where the salty sensation lies.

Take a brief moment to study and smell the treat: the pearlescent luster of the interior shell, the salty watery juices, the vibrant essence and then, quickly, slurp the prize. Let it flow down your throat. It's like drinking cool water, easy like standing still in a refreshing breeze. Then, after a momentary pause of appreciation, try another, and another. It is nice to share, to open a few for the other guests at the table, because eating oysters is rarely a private pleasure. You could of course use a fork, if you must, to assuage polite society. You could add a multitude of garnishes and trimmings: from the bright squeeze of citrus to the hot spike of pepper sauce, you could sprinkle mignonettes, herbs and spices, or then, cook it, letting the warm flavors explode in your mouth; it can be quite satisfying and delicious. Still, eating a fresh oyster raw, from the shell, is a rare, sacred and primal experience that fills one, as Hemingway noted, with hope and gratitude.

… with reverence. Like a child listening for the sea in a shell, eating a fresh oyster is like tasting the entire ocean. It is a fundamental flavor experience, like eating truffles or drinking a fine regional wine.

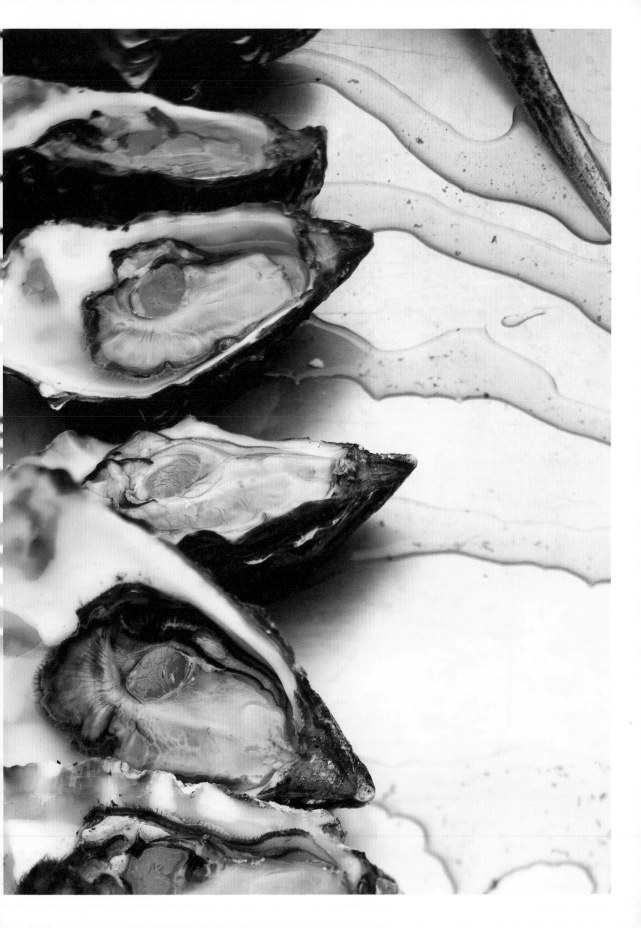

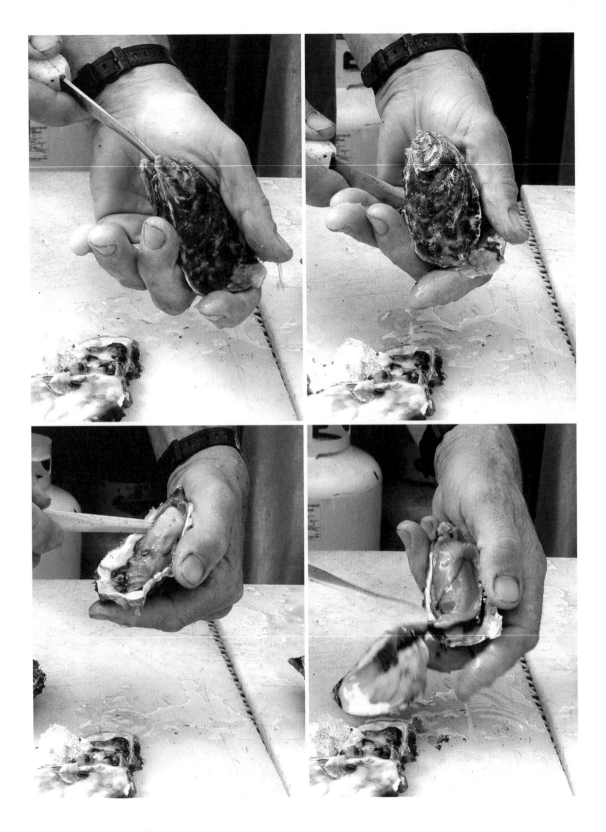

How to Open an Oyster

First, keep oysters on ice, never in water. Hold the oyster shell cup side down and insert the oyster knife into the top pivot point. Wiggle and twist the knife to break the hinge. Slide the knife down the right side of the shell, about two-thirds of the way down, to the abductor muscle. You will feel the resistance of the muscle against the knife. Sever the muscle and carefully lift the top shell, exposing the oyster meat. Slide the knife carefully loosening the meat from the muscle and the shell. Clear shell fragments using the tip of the knife. Serve.

A Note on Recipes

Oysters contain the taste of the ocean. One of the best ways to eat a fresh oyster is freshly shucked and raw, on the half shell, plain or with a squeeze of lemon and a dash of Tabasco. Aficionados relish slurping them down whole, savoring the oyster's texture and flavors. If you are wary at first, introduce your taste buds to the delicate and delicious flavors of oysters by eating them with a few sauces. Start with something simple like the classic mignonette and gradually add fruit or spice to it.

As oysters are a little salty, most sauce recipes do not call for any salt. Serve raw oysters on a bed of ice with chilled sauces. Always open oysters before barbequing. Although it may be tempting to sidestep the task of shucking, barbequing oysters in the whole shell will overcook them before you add sauces. Unless otherwise specified, the following recipes are based on four oysters per person. Adjust ingredient quantities accordingly.

For this "place-based" book it was only natural to us to suggest local wines for a chapter of oyster recipes. Sonoma is best known for its Pinot Noirs and Chardonnays. We've paired some of our favorites with the dishes here.

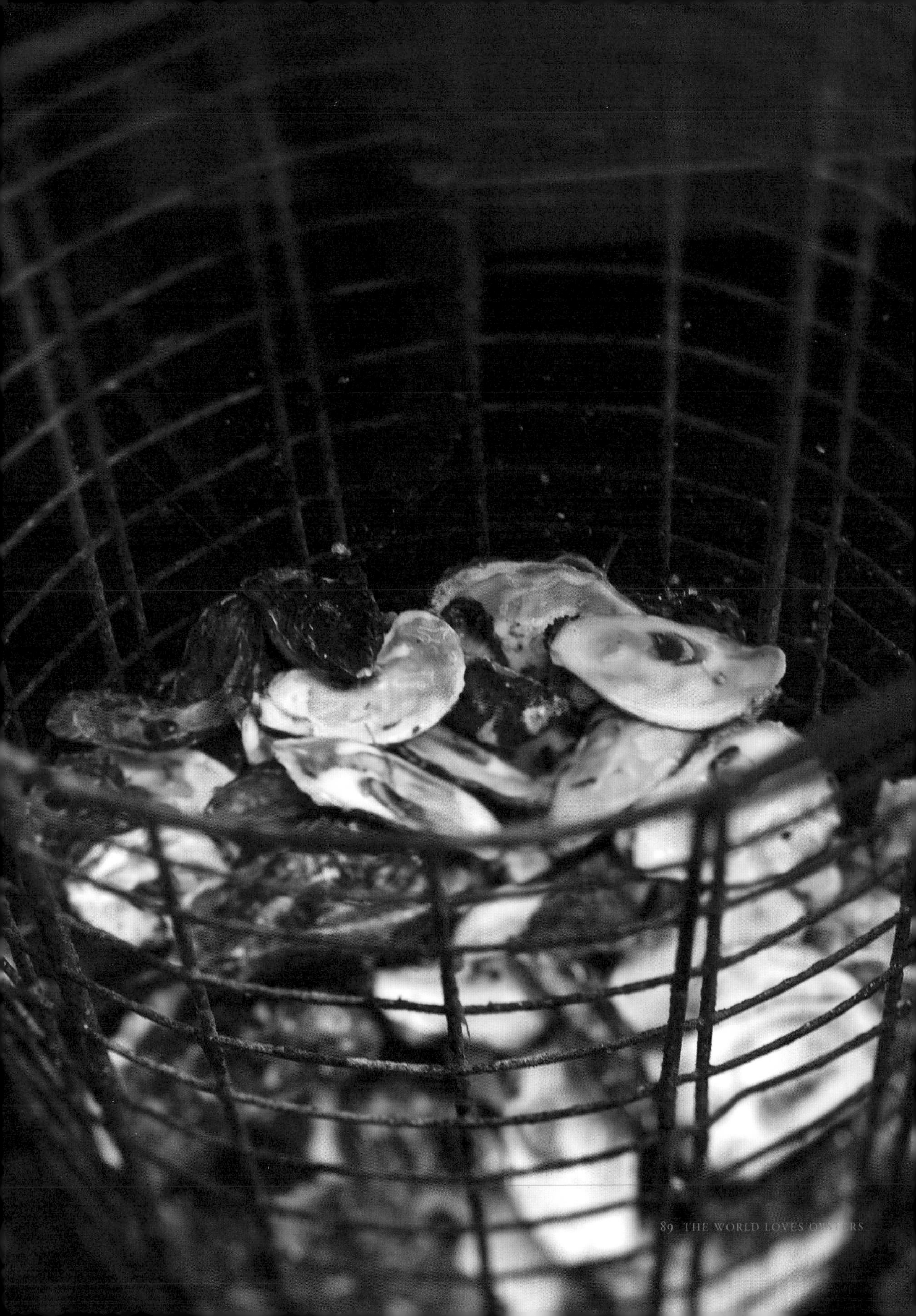

On the Half Shell

Mignonette is a classic French condiment, most commonly enjoyed with oysters. Culinarily "mignonette" means bundling together spices, peppercorns, and cloves and adding them to a dish for flavoring. Mignonette sauces use different types of vinegar but the common denominator is shallots and pepper.

Hog Island Oyster Company's famous "Hog Wash" mignonette has become Tomales Bay's best-known raw oyster sauce, to the extent that most local chefs now serve some variation of it. John Finger and Mike Watchorn, the company's owners, soon joined by a third partner, Terry Sawyer, started out with the goal of creating a high quality, sustainable practices oyster farm. In the process their business evolved into the area's most popular oyster farm. Mike developed the Hog Island Mignonette, known as Hog Wash, to complement the singular flavor of Tomales Bay oysters. With the Hog Island Traveling Oyster Bars, the partners created a new level of public contact and farmer-to-consumer oyster education: how they are grown, the importance of native oysters to the Tomales Bay ecosystem and, most importantly, how to enjoy them. Many of the area's other traveling oyster bars today are Hog Island-spawned.

Hog Island's Hog Wash

Makes enough for two dozen oysters

¼ cup peeled and finely diced shallot

1 large jalapeño pepper, seeded and finely diced

4 tablespoons finely chopped cilantro leaves

¼ cup seasoned rice vinegar

¼ cup natural rice vinegar

juice of 1 juicy lime

Mix shallots, jalapeño, and cilantro in a small bowl. Refrigerate if not using immediately. Mix rice vinegars together in a separate bowl. Shuck oysters, keeping as much of the liquid in the shell as possible. Place on a bed of ice on a deep-sided plate. Just before serving, spoon jalapeño mixture into a ramekin or small serving bowl, and pour the vinegar mixture up to the top of the ramekin. Place ramekin in the middle of the oysters and serve immediately, spooning a small amount on each oyster just before eating.

Mango Mignonette Sauce

From The Oyster Girls, a local traveling oyster bar affiliated with the Tomales Bay Oyster Company.

Makes enough for two dozen oysters

1 medium size, semi-firm but ripe mango, peeled and finely diced

¼ cup cilantro, finely chopped

½ cup seasoned rice vinegar

¼ cup freshly squeezed orange or tangerine juice

1 medium jalapeño pepper, seeded and minced finely

Combine all ingredients. Shuck oysters and serve as for the Hog Wash recipe.

Zesty Horseradish Sauce

Use fresh-grated horseradish if you can find it in your produce store for this colorful, refreshing sauce with a spicy kick. From The Oyster Girls.

Makes enough for two dozen oysters

1 tablespoon fresh horseradish root, peeled, rinsed, and grated (or 1 teaspoon store-bought horseradish)

¼ cup freshly juiced beet juice from washed and peeled beet

2 tablespoons freshly squeezed lemon juice

¼ cup seasoned rice vinegar

Mix beet and lemon juice with rice vinegar in a small bowl. Mix in horseradish. Keep chilled and airtight until ready to serve. Keeps for up to one week. Serve with oysters on the half shell.

Barbequed Oysters

TODAY THOUSANDS OF annual visitors to the Tomales Bay area buy oysters by the dozen to barbeque on the shore or at home, but that's a relatively new trend. Back when Jensen's Oyster Beds in the tiny town of Hamlet was farming and selling oysters in the 1950s, barbequed oysters were an oddity. In a *Point Reyes Light* article in 2000, Virginia Jensen recalls being kept busy all day, shucking over 100 dozen oysters for consumers who preferred jarred oysters to oysters in the shell.

RAW OR COOKED, oysters were not always as popular as they are today. It's said that you could once buy gunny sacks of them from Johnson's at Drakes Bay for a mere $15 a bag. But food trends change and barbequed oysters are now a sought-after and characteristic Tomales Bay regional food experience, greatly popular among the area's diverse groups of visitors. On any given weekend the picnic areas of the Tomales Bay and Hog Island oyster companies are filled with picnickers, their tables and accoutrements a picture of the diverse cultures that love eating the oyster.

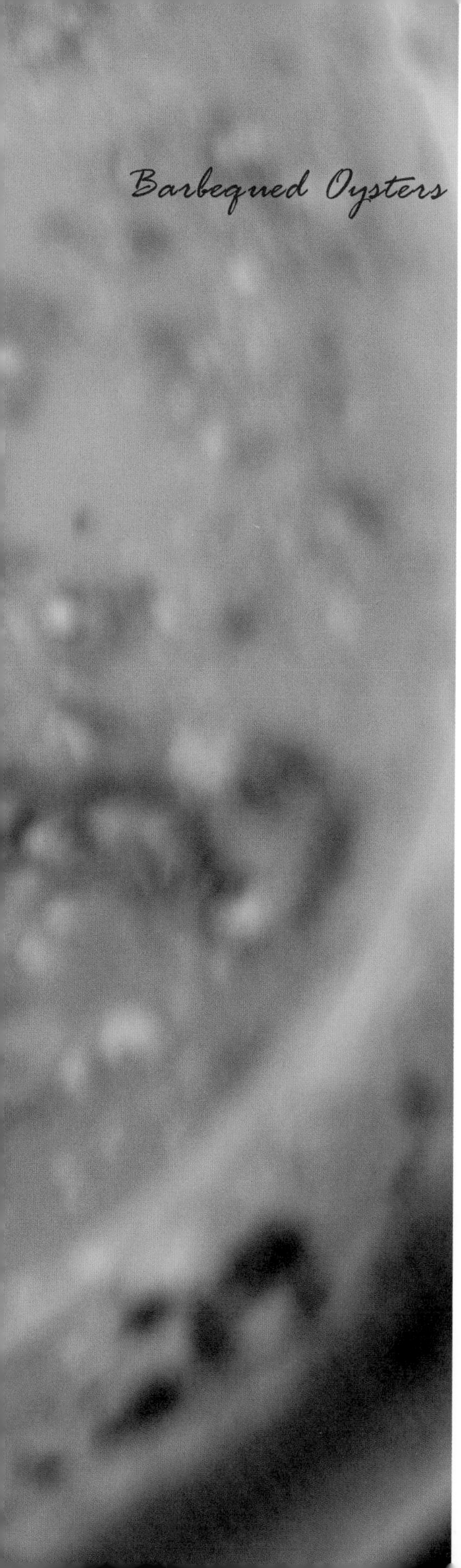

Barbequed Oysters with Garlic Butter

24 oysters

1 cup unsalted butter

3 tablespoons minced garlic

juice of 1 lemon

salt and pepper to taste

Preheat the grill. In a small saucepan, melt the butter. Then add garlic and cook for about one minute. Add the lemon juice, stir and set aside. You can cool and refrigerate if not using immediately. It will keep for up to a week.

Shuck oysters and place them directly on a preheated grill, keeping as much of the oyster liquid in the shell as possible. This will prevent them from drying out and add to the dish's flavor. Spoon on a teaspoon of garlic butter, cover and cook until the sauce bubbles. If using a broiler instead of a grill, keep at a low heat (250º) and place oysters on one inch of rock salt (also known as ice cream salt) on a baking dish. Keep rack at least 12 inches from the broiler. If the oven is too hot and the oysters are too close to the heat, the oyster shell, which contains water, can pop, causing splinters to fall into the oyster meat. When butter sauce bubbles, remove from heat and add barbeque sauce before serving.

Anastacio's Famous

Anastacio Gonzalez (or just "Anastacio" as he is better known) had never even seen an oyster large enough to barbeque until he was presented with a sack of them one summer evening in 1972 at the Tomales Bay Sportsmen's Association's "Shark and Ray Derby." At the end of the day he and his fellow fisherman were cooking their catches at Nick's Cove, where they convened every evening during the two-day annual event.

That evening Anastacio also didn't know what to do with the oysters, so he threw them on the grill along with the shark and stingray he was grilling. Thinking the suggested butter and salt accompaniment a bit bland, he concocted a sauce based on one his mother served with barbequed shrimp back in his Mexican hometown of Valle de Guadalupe. (Well over a tenth of West Marin's population is Latino, many of whom come from three small cities near Guadalajara: Valle de Guadalupe, San Miguel el Alto, and Jalostotitlan.)

Oysters were eaten raw on the half shell at the time, and Anastacio's novelty preparation was a hit. He continued to cook it up for a dedicated following at Nick's Cove and later at Tony's Seafood and the Marshall Tavern. Over the years he became a master griller, perfecting the art of grilling to order—medium, or medium rare—as many as 4,500 oysters in three hours using a customized Weber grill. In 1980, when Sunset magazine featured Anastacio, the "inventor" of the West Marin barbequed oysters trend, his fame spread well beyond the region.

In 2009, Anastacio's Famous BBQ Oyster Sauce was introduced and is now available throughout California. While the ingredients that appear on the label are also listed here, Anastacio does not disclose quantities on the label—or here. "It adds to the mystique," he says, smiling.

The ingredients: unsalted tomato paste, whi wine, garlic, sugar, brown sugar, distilled vinegar, soy sauce, salt, garlic, onion, parsley and spices.

Anastacio and Luis prepare their famous
Barbecued
Drake's Bay Oysters

at the
MARSHALL
TAVERN

Saturday and Sunday noon-8 p.m.

663-8141 COAST HIGHWAY ONE MARSHALL

The Marshall Store BBQ Sauce

Makes enough for two
dozen oysters

1 cup ketchup
¼ cup Marshall Store Janis's
Chipotle Sauce
1-2 cloves minced garlic
1 tablespoon horseradish
juice of 2 juicy limes
salt and pepper to taste

Blend all ingredients in Cuisinart
until smooth and evenly blended.

Janis's Chipotle Sauce

7 ounce can of chipotle
peppers in Adobe sauce
(available
in Mexican grocery store or
Mexican section of grocery
store)
¼ cup of molasses
¼ cup of distilled vinegar
½ cup water
sprinkle of salt

Blend all ingredients in Cuisinart
until smooth and evenly blended.
Makes two cups.

The Marshall Store

THE MARSHALL STORE has had two locations and many incarnations during its 136 years of existence. It first started at the Marshall Train depot as a general store (with a poolroom), located where Hog Island Oyster Company stands today. The Store also served as the school bus stop for local kids. Today's Marshall Store next to the Boat Works was started as a sandwhich shop by Jacqui Villich. Kathy Krohn later turned the Store into an eclectic café with terrariums filled with turtles, rare frogs, and koi and hanging plants. Her sign, "Best Oysters on the Planet," was a roadside fixture for seven years. Heidi and Shannon Gregory and Kim Laboa now run it as an oyster bar, serving delicious fare in a superb location overlooking the bay's harbor. Shannon, an Australian native and French-trained chef, includes smoked meats and varied seafood dishes on the menu.

The Marshall Store Oysters Rockefeller

According to culinary lore, this rich and flavorful dish is named Rockefeller because it is green, the color of money. Variations substitute yogurt for some of the cheese, or chard for the spinach.

Serves six

2 tablespoons olive oil

1 cup breadcrumbs

3 cups cooked spinach, chopped, with water squeezed out

½ small red onion, diced

2 cups plain yogurt

1 cup grated Parmesan cheese

¾ cup of grated Gruyere cheese

¼ teaspoon freshly grated nutmeg

¼ teaspoon ground anise seed or 2 tablespoons Pernod

salt and pepper to taste

24 medium oysters

Preheat oven or grill.

Toast breadcrumbs over medium heat in two tablespoons olive oil, stirring often until breadcrumbs are evenly toasted. In a large bowl mix all other ingredients. Set aside.

Shuck oysters, keeping as much liquid in the shell as possible (this adds flavor and helps cheese melt faster). Leaving each oyster in its half shell, put a tablespoon of mixture on top of each one and top with breadcrumbs. Place an ovenproof plate or platter with a layer of rock salt about 1-inch deep (moisten the salt very slightly) on a grill or in the oven. Set oysters in the rock salt, making sure they are level. Cook until the cheese is melted, then carefully remove from oven or grill. Serve hot.

Freestone Vineyards' Fogdog Chardonnay
Melon, apricot and Meyer lemon flavors match well with this rich, classic oyster dish. Sonoma Coast AVA.

Oysters with Chorizo Butter

Fom the Marshall Store

Serves six

¼ pound fresh Mexican chorizo, removed from casing

1 cup unsalted butter, softened

2 tablespoons finely chopped parsley

24 oysters, shucked, in shell

Soften butter at room temperature. Sauté chorizos until thoroughly cooked, then crumble. Place in refrigerator to cool. Place butter in a small bowl and break up with a wooden spoon. Add cooled chorizo and mix thoroughly. Add parsley. Place the mixture in the middle of a sheet of waxed paper. Roll into a 2-inch wide log, tie ends of plastic wrap and cool in refrigerator until firm. Place opened oysters on grill and top with a thin-sliced round of butter cut from roll. Cover and cook just until the butter starts to bubble.

Oysters with Pesto Butter Sauce

From the Oyster Girls

Serves six

½ pound unsalted butter

1 leek, cut lengthways, washed and sliced into ¼ inch pieces

2 cloves garlic, minced

½ cup pesto

½ lemon, optional

¼ cup of beer, optional

24 oysters, shucked, in shell

Melt two tablespoons of butter on low heat. Add the leek and sauté on medium heat until it becomes translucent, being careful not to burn the butter. Add the rest of the butter and melt on low heat. Stir constantly. Add the garlic and pesto, and stir until well mixed. Turn off heat and add lemon and beer, if desired. Cover an ovenproof plate or platter with a layer of rock salt about 1-inch deep (moisten the salt very slightly). Set oysters in the rock salt, making sure they are level. Spoon the sauce on the oysters. Place in oven on broil. If barbequing oysters, place opened oysters on grill and spoon butter on each oyster. Cover grill and cook until bubbling.

Shannon's Smoked Oyster Crostini

Serves eight

Smoked Oysters

Mesquite wood chips, soaked in water for 20 minutes, then drained

3 dozen medium to large oysters in the shell

juice of 6 lemons, preferably Meyer lemons

2 tablespoons olive oil

1 sprig thyme, finely minced

1 tablespoon fresh-ground black pepper

Start up grill with mesquite charcoal. Once coals are burning spread some in a circle around the outside of the grill and the rest in the center. Cover the ones in the center with aluminum foil. In a large bowl, toss shucked oysters in the lemon juice and place on grill. Place the lid on the grill, and open the vent enough to create airflow. Cook until the oysters are firm, about 45 minutes to one hour. In a large bowl mix the olive oil and pepper. Remove oysters from shell and toss in the olive oil mixture.

Crostini

1 baguette, preferably good quality sourdough

2 tablespoons olive oil

1 tablespoon fresh-ground black pepper and salt to taste

Preheat the oven to 350°. Diagonally slice the baguette into ¼-inch pieces. Mix the olive oil and pepper in a small bowl. Place slices on baking sheet and drizzle with olive oil-pepper mixture and season with additional pepper and salt, to taste. Place slices in the oven until they are evenly toasted.

Chipotle Aioli

2 tablespoons mayonnaise

¼ tablespoon of Janis's Chipotle sauce

1 tablespoon of diced pickle

Mix 2 tablespoons mayonnaise with ¼ tablespoon of Janis's Chipotle sauce (p. 103) and 1 tablespoon of diced pickle. To serve, spoon an oyster onto a slice of toasted baguette, top with aioli, and garnish with thyme and black pepper.

Sixteen by Twenty Vineyard Gap's Crown Chardonney

The flavors of lemon peel, pear, and spicy oak are a delicious match for this dish's smoky oyster flavor and chipotle aoili kick. Sonoma Coast AVA.

The Marshall Store Fish Stew

Serves six to eight

1 clove garlic, minced

3 pounds clams

3 tablespoons olive oil

1 medium onion, diced

1 leek, cut lengthways, washed and sliced into ¼-inch pieces

1 medium-size fennel bulb, outer leaves removed, cored and sliced into ¼-inch pieces

1 Andouille sausage, thinly sliced

14-ounce can crushed tomatoes

2 medium-size red potatoes, peeled and cubed

1 Poblano or Pasilla chili

1 tablespoon Espelette pepper or other good-quality pimento powder

1 teaspoon chili powder

1 pound fresh rock cod or halibut, cut into 1-inch cubes

½ pound Dungeness crab meat

Wash clams and place in large pot with 2½ cups water and the garlic. Cover and steam until clams are opened. Drain liquid into a small bowl and set liquid and clams aside. Roast pepper on a flame, turning often until skin is black. Place in a brown bag for a few minutes so pepper can sweat and will be easier to peel. Remove from bag and peel off the charred skin, cut lengthways and remove seeds. Dice into small pieces. Set aside. Sauté the onions in the olive oil until they are translucent. Add leeks and fennel and sauté until slightly browned. Add the Andouille sausage and cook for a few more minutes, then add the clam juice, followed by the tomatoes and three cups of water. Add the potatoes, Pasilla chili, pimento powder, and chili powder and bring to a boil, then lower heat and simmer. When potatoes are almost cooked add the clams in the shell, fish and crab and simmer for a half hour. Season to taste with salt.

Radio-Coteau's Pinot Noir "La Neblina"
A dark red fruit and spice palate stands up to this hearty fish stew's robust sausage, fish and pepper flavors. Sonoma Coast AVA.

Oysters Kilpatrick

An Australian recipe that has migrated to Tomales Bay, it has pronounced and complementary flavors and is quick and easy to make at home. From the Marshall Store.

Serves six

8 ounces Applewood smoked bacon, cut into ½-inch strips

¼ cup Worcestershire sauce

½ cup ketchup

24 oysters, shucked, in shell

1 lemon

1 tablespoon parsley, cleaned, dried and finely chopped

Turn oven to broil or start grill. Sauté bacon until almost cooked. Mix Worcestershire sauce and ketchup.

Cover an ovenproof plate or platter with a layer of rock salt about 1-inch deep (moisten the salt very slightly). Set oysters in the rock salt, making sure they are level. Spoon sauce on each oyster and top with bacon. If barbequing oysters, place opened oysters on grill and spoon 1 teaspoon of sauce, then bacon on each oyster. Cover grill. Cook until bacon is browned and cooked through. Serve hot with a squeeze of lemon and garnish with chopped parsley.

Indian Peach Catering Co.'s Po' Boy

Serves four

For the "dredge"

½ cup wheat flour

½ cup corn meal

2 tablespoons rice flour

3 tablespoons cornstarch

1 teaspoon each salt, black pepper and paprika

¼ teaspoon cayenne

12 oysters

2 cups corn oil for deep-frying

4 white hot dog buns

For the remoulade

½ cup mayonnaise

2 tablespoons finely diced capers

2 tablespoons finely diced shallots

2 tablespoons finely diced cornichons

2 tablespoons parsley, stems removed, washed, dried and finely chopped

zest of 1 medium-size lemon

juice of 1 medium-size juicy lemon

A dash or 3 of your favorite hot sauce and black pepper

1 lemon

¼ cup of chopped parsley

Mix wheat flour, corn meal, rice flour, and cornstarch together well. Add salt, fresh ground pepper, paprika and cayenne and mix well. Wash and open oysters, discard the shells and set aside. Put oysters in "dredge" mixture and cover well. Shake off any excess and put in refrigerator to set for an hour. Heat oil slowly in a deep pan until hot but not smoking. Fry gently in hot oil, turning once and loosening oysters from the bottom of the pan if they are stuck. Fry until golden and crisp. Using a slotted spoon, remove from oil and place on a paper towel or waxed paper to drain. Place two to three oysters in a buttered hot dog or morning bun with a heaping tablespoon of remoulade on top. Garnish with a squeeze of lemon and sprinkling of parsley.

County Line Anderson Valley Rosé
A pale, silvery pink-toned wine with mineral notes that highlight this remoulade twist on the classic po' boy. Anderson Valley AVA.

Osteria Stellina Oyster Pizza

Makes two eight-inch round pizzas

The creamy leek sauce in this recipe replaces the cheese and sauce of a traditional pizza.

The simple dough recipe makes a fine crisp, thin pizza crust. As Osteria Stellina chef Christian Caiazzo poetically puts it, "The water temperature (for the dough) is very important: mimic the temperature of water that is collected in a tub within a stone building that gets no direct sun."

Pizza dough

4 cups of "00" Caputo flour or Giusto's or other high-protein baker's flour

1 cup cold water

½ ounce yeast

1 tablespoon salt

Mix yeast and water briefly in Kitchen Aid. Pour mixture into a small bowl and let sit for five minutes. Stir in one cup of flour, incorporating it slowly. Let sit for five minutes, then add the salt and mix quickly. Add the rest of the flour and mix. Turn out onto a floured surface and knead until dough is smooth. Let rest for five minutes. If the dough feels too wet to the touch, add a small amount of flour. Place dough in a plastic container and cover. Refrigerate for four hours until dough has doubled in size. Remove dough from refrigerator and divide into two small rounds. Roll into balls. Let the dough rise again for two to four hours until it has doubled again in size.

Leek Sauce

3 tablespoons butter

1 tablespoon olive oil

3 leeks, cut in half, washed and sliced into ¼-inch crescents

salt and pepper to taste

2 sprigs of lemon thyme, lightly chopped

1 tablespoon of Italian (or flat) parsley, washed, dried and chopped

2 cups of heavy cream

Warm a medium-size, thick-bottomed sauté pan and add the butter and oil. Add the leeks when the oil mixture is fairly hot but not smoking. Cook until leeks are soft and translucent, season with salt and pepper. Add the lemon thyme and one tablespoon of chopped parsley. Turn off heat and add the cream, then cook on medium to low heat until mixture reaches a creamy, sauce-like consistency, approximately ten minutes. The sauce should not be overly thick, as it will thicken more as it cools. Set sauce aside to cool.
Continues on page 120.

Kendric Vineyards Pinot Noir
Warm cherry, dried rose, plum and tobacco notes pair up well with the pizza's creamy leeks and oysters. Marin County AVA.

16 oysters

Shuck oysters, and set aside on a plate out of the shell

For the pizza

¼ cup olive oil

2 tablespoons of Italian (or flat) parsley, washed, dried and chopped

1 teaspoon crushed chili flakes

Preheat oven to 550°.

Flatten the two pizza dough rounds into a round, thin pizza shape. Lightly brush each with extra virgin olive oil, covering the whole top of each pizza as this helps the crust get crispy. Evenly sprinkle each pizza with salt and pepper, the parsley and chilies. Spread the leek mixture onto each pizza up to about half an inch from the edge, spreading it quickly and gently so the dough doesn't get too warm or torn. Place eight oysters on each pizza, one for each slice, working in a circular motion. Slide pizza immediately into pizza oven or onto a pizza stone and then into the oven. Bake until very crispy, approximately eight minutes. Garnish with remaining parsley, cut each pizza into eight pieces, and serve immediately.

Pfendler Vineyards Pinot Noir Rosé

This wine's bright salmon hue, and opulent notes of raspberry, watermelon, kumquat and spice make an attractive accompaniment to the Tartare's clean, bright flavors. Sonoma Coast AVA.

Oyster and Tuna Tartare

From Nicks Cove

Serves six

2 small to medium oysters, opened, removed
from shell and chopped

2 ounces Ahi tuna, sushi grade, finely diced

4 chives, chopped

½ tablespoon extra virgin olive oil

zest of ½ lemon

sea salt to taste (preferably Maldon)

4 slices of a good-quality baguette, brushed
with olive oil, and lightly grilled or toasted

Combine all ingredients, except for bread, and mix well
with a spoon. Spoon mixture onto slices of baguette and
sprinkle with chives and sea salt.

Stellina Tomales Cove Mussels

Serves four to six as an appetizer

1 pound Tomales Cove or fresh mussels

3 tablespoons olive oil

½ tablespoon garlic

pinch crushed chilies

¼ medium Walla Walla, Maui, or Vidalia onion,
in ¼-inch slices

½ red pepper, in ¼-inch slices

½ cup spicy sausage, cut into bite-size pieces

2 tablespoons finely chopped Italian parsley

¼ cup white cooking wine

1 cup fish stock or shellfish stock (use chicken stock
or water if unavailable)

sea salt and fresh-ground black pepper to taste

1 fresh baguette or country-style bread with good crust

Wash mussels and drain well. De-beard mussels by pulling "hairs" out of end of mussel shell.

Heat a deep sauté pan over a medium flame. Add olive oil, garlic and chilies, sautéing until evenly cooked. Add the onion. Cook until transparent, and then add the red pepper. Stir well and season the vegetables. Add the spicy sausage, stir and then add mussels. Toss and stir the mussels through mixture. Add 1 tablespoon of parsley and sauté, tossing mussels in pan often to develop a rich flavor. Add white wine and cook until it is reduced by half. Shake the pan and add the stock. Cook to meld the flavors of the broth until all mussels are opened fully. Season the broth and mussels again with salt and pepper, add remaining tablespoon of chopped parsley for a fresh herb flavor and serve immediately with crusty bread in warm bowls.

Pey Marin Vineyards Shell Mound Riesling
This tiny vineyard's cool coastal position and well-drained marine sandstone soil give a brisk acidity and bright green apple and slate flavors. Marin County AVA.

Nick's Cove Oysters Mornay

Serves six

4 tablespoons unsalted butter

1 tablespoon shallot, finely minced

1 heaping tablespoon all-purpose flour

½ cup white wine

1 cup milk

½ cup heavy cream

½ cup Gruyere, grated

½ cup Parmigiano Reggiano, grated

1 sprig thyme, finely minced

3-4 drops Tabasco sauce

coarse black pepper

2 teaspoons toasted breadcrumbs

24 medium-size oysters, shucked, in shell

Melt butter with shallots in a saucepan, then whisk in flour. Cook flour and butter for about two minutes on medium heat, whisking often until smooth. Turn down heat, mix in wine and then add milk. Cook and stir constantly for a few minutes, until milk mixture thickens to almost a paste consistency. Add cream and cheese (reserve a tablespoon of Parmigiano Reggiano) and cook until cheese is melted into mixture. Add thyme, Tabasco sauce, and season with pepper. Turn oven onto broil. Cover an ovenproof plate or platter with a layer of rock salt about 1-inch deep (moisten the salt very slightly). Set oysters in the rock salt, making sure they are level. Spoon sauce on each oyster and top with breadcrumbs and remaining cheese. Broil until top is golden brown. Be careful not to overcook the oysters. Serve hot.

Clary Ranch Vineyard's Pinot Noir
Flavors of ripe raspberry, plenty of spice, bright cherry, blackberry and plum stand up superbly to the Mornay's rich, cheesy topping. Sonoma Coast AVA.

Oysters in Sparkling Wine

This recipe is from Drakes Bay Oyster Company, the last operating oyster cannery in California. Using homemade breadcrumbs adds more flavor than packaged breadcrumbs, mainly because they are fresh and have no added ingredients.

Serves six

½ quart of small freshly canned Drakes Bay oysters

(approximately 18 oysters)

4 tablespoons unsalted cup butter

½ cup Sparkling wine

¼ cup toasted fine breadcrumbs

1 tablespoon washed, dried and finely chopped parsley

fresh ground pepper

1 loaf bread, white or brown, sliced, with crusts removed

2 tablespoons unsalted butter for bread

Preheat oven to 300º. Melt butter on the stove and pour half of it into two-inch baking dish. Arrange the oysters in two layers on the butter and baste them with the remaining melted butter. Sprinkle the oysters with breadcrumbs, parsley, and ground pepper. Pour the wine over them. Cook until oysters become plump, the edges fluted and crinkly and the breadcrumbs golden brown, about 25 minutes. The sauce should not be boiling or bubbling. While oysters are cooking toast slices of French bread and spread with butter. Serve oysters at once with the toast, a green salad and the rest of that bottle of Sparkling Wine.

Iron Horse Vineyard's Blanc de Blancs

This most elegant of wines has lemon, green apple, and orange blossom aromas and flavors. From the Green Valley AVA, one of the smallest viticultural areas in Sonoma County.

Tempura Oysters

A Valentine's Day special from the Station House

Serves four

Batter

½ cup cornstarch

1 cup all-purpose flour

2 cups Canola oil for deep frying

1½ cups Champagne

Wakame Salad

1 ounce dried wakame seaweed

¼ cup rice vinegar

2 tablespoons grapeseeed, Canola or neutral flavored oil

1 teaspoon sea salt

1 tablespoon honey

red pepper flakes to taste

2 tablespoons toasted sesame seeds

Dipping Sauce

2 tablespoons soy sauce

2 tablespoons seasoned rice wine vinegar

2 tablespoons mirin

1 teaspoon chili flakes

2 scallions, sliced thinly and diagonally

Mix cornstarch and flour. Add sparkling wine and stir briskly to get rid of all lumps. The consistancy should be between a crepe and pancake batter. Add more Champagne if necessary. Set aside for 30 minutes.

Rehydrate wakame in a bowl of water for five minutes. Drain and rinse. In a small bowl, mix rice vinegar, oil, sesame oil salt and sugar. Add red pepper flakes and sesame seeds. Toss wakame in mixture. Set aside.

Shuck the oysters, saving the shells. Heat oil until hot but not smoking. Dip the oyster in the batter and fry, loosening the oysters from bottom of pan if necessary, until the batter starts to turn golden. To serve, place a small heap of wakame salad on the empty shell. Place tempura oyster on top, and serve with dipping sauce.

The Station House Oyster Stew

Serves four

2 cooked red potatoes, cut into 1-inch cubes

1 tablespoon olive oil

2 tablespoons unsalted butter

2 leeks, sliced lengthways, washed and cut into ¼-inch crescents

1 cup sliced cremini mushrooms

¼ cup dry white wine

dash of Tabasco

12 small to medium oysters, shucked

2 cups chopped Swiss chard

1 tablespoon garlic compound butter

3 cups heavy cream

2 tablespoons chopped tarragon

1 tablespoon finely chopped parsley

compound garlic butter

salt

Compound Garlic Butter

¼ cup softened unsalted butter

1 tablespoon minced garlic

Mix softened butter and garlic well with a wooden spoon. Place on a piece of waxed paper and roll. Refrigerate.

Parboil potatoes until done. Drain and set aside. Heat oil and butter in a heavy-bottomed pan. Sauté the leeks and mushrooms until the mushrooms start to brown and the leeks soften. Add 2 tablespoons white wine and Tabasco. Then add oysters, potato and chard with 2 tablespoons of the compound butter. When the butter has melted and the chard has wilted, add the remaining wine and cream. Simmer on low heat until the cream has thickened. Add tarragon and salt to taste. Serve hot.

Hartford Court's Fog Dance Vineyards Pinot Noir

Shows lots of lovely Bing cherry, allspice, black and red currant notes and a pronounced minerality, making it a top choice for this creamy oyster stew accented with greens and mushrooms. Russian River Valley AVA.

a conservation timeline

It is no accident that Tomales Bay remains scenically unspoilt and undeveloped. In the 1960s, a growing environmental movement fought to protect this valuable open space that was in jeopardy of being encroached upon by growing urban populations. Point Reyes National Seashore and the Golden Gate Recreation Area were established to protect Tomales Bay, Point Reyes Peninsula seashore, and its esteros and beaches. The Audubon Society, Sierra Club, National Parks Service and various citizens' groups successfully lobbied to protect the area for recreational use, scientific research, and environmental education. Today the area's coexistence of wetland and public lands with farms illustrates how protecting the seashore and Bay waters can benefit both communities and commerce.

Marin's outstanding model of farmer stewardship is a national benchmark for achieving conservation goals. What made this possible is largely the community's investment in cultural continuity and a relationship with the land. Farmers here remain on their properties through successive generations. Ranchers are closely involved with watershed management, including restoring thousands of acres of riparian habitat. This stewardship requires patience and a long-term conservation approach—practices grounded in a long-term commitment to the land that gradually become part of a communal culture.

58- 1964   Tomales Bay narrowly escaped becoming a neighbor to a nuclear reactor when PG&E announced plans for an atomic park in Bodega Bay in 1961, one of two such parks proposed for northern California. The other, Eureka, site was built, but in Bodega Bay there was vigorous opposition. Even when residents, scientists, and the Point Reyes-based anti-nuclear group, the Pelican Alliance, pointed out that the proposed plant's location was just a few hundred feet from the San Andreas Fault, near Bodega Head, PG&E persisted, breaking ground before development was stopped. Today the abandoned construction site is a duck pond, referred to by locals as "the Hole in the Head."

1962   Point Reyes National Seashore (PRNS) was established through the efforts of environmentally aware local residents, parks service employees and organizations like the Sierra Club. Thousands of acres were purchased with public funds and protected for public recreation.

1967   The 1967 West Marin General Plan was an aggressive pro-growth initiative put forward by a developer-friendly Marin County Board of Supervisors. Their plan was to divide land surrounding Tomales Bay into a dense suburban area of a quarter million people on two-acre lots with highway access and scenic highways. These proposed suburbs would have threatened the natural ecosystem and covered the West Marin hillsides with houses. The increased population would have destroyed the fishing and aquaculture industries in the Tomales Bay and Drakes Estero and threatened the economic viability of West Marin farmland.

1970   The privately-funded Audubon Canyon Ranch purchased land along the Tomales Bay shore to protect it from development. Their first two aquisitions in 1970 were four acres at Shields Marsh in Inverness and twenty acres of Oscar Johannson's oyster tidelands, protecting Cypress Grove, near Marshall.

1971   The Environmental Action Committee (EAC) of West Marin was founded by a group of citizens who wanted both to protect the region from immediate threats and to foster a wider understanding of its unique qualities. One of EAC's early battles was over a plan to dike the southern end of Tomales Bay and destroy its tidal wetlands. The group organized a well-publicized "sail-in" of local boats that drew attention to the scheme and mobilized public opposition to it. The campaign was successful and the dike was cancelled. In the same year, EAC was an important voice in the chorus of criticism that ultimately killed the county's West Marin General Plan.

1971 A newly elected, environmentally aware and agriculture-friendly board, realizing that development would endanger the existence of communities and ecosystems, moved to repeal the 1967 West Marin General Plan. The plan was opposed by the Marin Conservation League, Marin County Farm Bureau, Tomales Bay Association, the Marin Alternative and the EAC.

1971 East Marin's shore remained vulnerable to development as long as ranchers could subdivide and sell land. At the time there was a lot of pressure to do so: the drop in milk prices put dairy farmers under increasing economic strain, and the area was becoming overpopulated as urban areas rapidly expanded.

Realizing that these pressures endangered farmland, the Board of Supervisors moved to preserve West Marin agricultural areas by implementing a controversial "A-60" parcel size limitation: only one home could be built on sixty acres.

Not everyone in the ranching community supported this zoning law. In her comprehensive survey "Tomales Bay Environmental History and Historic Resource Study," Christy Avery illustrates this opposition in a quote from local rancher Earl Dolcini: "They would like to see us remain as ranches so when they take their Sunday drive we're the picture in the middle of their imaginary frame." Despite resistance, two thirds of the lands surrounding Tomales Bay were zoned A-60.

1971 West Marin residents, whether full-time or in summer, who live along or close to the Bay have at times been its greatest stewards. Their efforts to preserve the Bay have, in at least one case, affected national resource management policy. Inverness resident Peter Whitney won a landmark decision against developer Larry Marks over Marks's Chicken Ranch beach property that he wanted to develop into a marina. This tideland and beach on the Tomales Bay's western shore is a popular swimming spot.

Whitney, a longtime resident who had a family home on the beach, gathered support from the Inverness Waterfront Committee and the Sierra Club to oppose Marks's plan. Marks sued Whitney in response. The California Supreme Court decision ruling in Whitney's favor made a significant clarification to the application of the Public Trust Doctrine (PTD). Until 1971, the PTD had functioned according to Roman law: holding in public trusts the common resources of air, water, sea and shore for the public's commercial use. The doctrine was first incorporated in American resource management in the 1800s to allow for the improvement and expansion of oyster beds in New Jersey's Raritan. Navigation, fishing and aquaculture industries were its primary beneficiaries.

This ruling on the use of public trust tidelands was later updated to include the protection of tidelands as publicly held ecological zones to be preserved for scientific and recreational use. It emphasized the connection between ecological value and public use and included on its list not only navigable rivers but also small streams, setting a precedent for future coastal development.

1972   The establishment of the Golden Gate Recreation Area put Tomales Bay permanently on the map as a conserved, scenic recreation destination. Recreational use is defined as environmentally sensitive activities like kayaking, sailing and windsurfing.

1972   The Coastal Zone Initiative was passed to establish the California Coastal Commission.

1976   Legislation passed to create the Point Reyes Wilderness, named after Representative Phillip Burton in 1985, who first introduced the bill in 1971. It included nearly half of the Point Reyes National Seashore.

1980   The agricultural conservation movement continued. Marin Agriculture Land Trust (MALT), founded by residents Phyllis Faber and Ellen Straus, added its support by purchasing individual development rights. Since the 1980s the group has acquired thousands of acres of West Marin agriculture lands.

1988   Point Reyes was included in the Golden Gate Biosphere Reserve by The United Nations Biosphere Program. It was the first U.S. biosphere reserve incorporating a densely populated urban area.

1994   Albert Straus established Straus Family Creamery, the first organic dairy west of the Mississippi River, in Marshall.

2002   Tomales Bay was added to The Ramsar List of Wetlands of International Importance, which recognizes those wetlands that "contain a representative, rare, or unique example of a natural or near-natural wetland type."

2007   Another significant contribution to the protection and sustainability of the Tomales Bay ecosystem was the completion of phase one of the Giacomini Wetlands Restoration Project. Five hundred and sixty acres of former grazing land at the Bay's southern end were restored to original tidal wetlands, adding 4% to the existing wetland acreage in coastal California.

2007   The Vermont National Park Service Conservation Study Institute issued a groundbreaking report on rethinking management of public land, called Stewardship Begins with People. It recognized the increasing threats farmers face in their social and economic relationship to the land, and that food production on publicly managed lands relies on partnerships and collaborations to reconcile production with environmental conservation. It also cited place-based products as models for protecting cultural and economic sustainability in distinctive regions. Point Reyes and West Marin are used as examples of "places of quality production and authentic foods." The report looks at place-based products as models for protecting cultural and economic sustainability in distinctive regions. The report states of the West Marin area: "An unusual opportunity exists to demonstrate the powerful linkage between these innovative, sustainable agriculture enterprises, market recognition and the continued, careful stewardship of an important cultural landscape." Hog Island Oyster Company, Cowgirl Creamery, Marin Sun Farms and Strauss Diary are named in the report.

"An opportunity exists to demonstrate the powerful linkage between innovative, sustainable agriculture enterprises, market recognition and careful stewardship of an important cultural landscape."

Coming Changes

While the threat of suburban developments is under control and demand for oysters remains constant, there are other factors that will ultimately alter the Tomales Bay area ecosystem and community. In 2004 an alarming thing occurred in West Coast oyster hatcheries: the Pacific oyster failed to reproduce. This trend continued from 2004 to 2008 and affected all West Coast oyster growers dependent upon the hatcheries for their seed. Once disease was ruled out, it was determined that ocean acidification was the cause. The ocean has a downwelling and upwelling system, in which carbon dioxide enters the ocean, travels to the bottom and then cycles back up in a seasonal upwelling, a process that takes approximately fifty years. The upwelling systems that we are now experiencing contain atmospheric carbon levels from the 1960s. But the ocean's chemistry has changed due to the increase of carbon dioxide, and even if we significantly reduce our carbon output today, the output over the last 200 years will still continue to make the ocean more acidic.

This acidification trend affects the shallow waters of coastal estuarine systems more acutely than it does the deep ocean. Acidic or under-saturated waters are corrosive to shellfish or calcifying organisms, which need the opposite—alkaline conditions—to develop their shells. Shellfish have survived for millions of years by adapting to environmental changes but may not be able to do so quickly enough this time. This does not bode well for the entire food chain, as shellfish are a primary food source linking fish, whales, seabirds and humans.

Scientists are now trying to evaluate short-term and long-term offsets for carbon build-up. Environmental management on an ecosystem level, such as seeding the ocean with iron, is a massive manipulation of the environment that may be able to slow down the acidification process. The obvious long-term solution to this problem is to reduce drastically our use of carbon-based fuels. Oyster farmers are unable to predict how or to what degree these environmental changes will affect their livelihoods. Farmers are actively involved with marine scientists and biologists, tracking and transmitting visible changes, but their reports cannot influence how acidification will affect oyster populations. To make predictions even more difficult, fluctuating populations are a natural phenomena that make it hard to identify a benchmark of ocean acidification against which to measure current levels in the future. "All we can do right now," says Terry Sawyer of Hog Island Oyster Company, "is track and communicate with each other." What is clear is that the effects of ocean acidification will be experienced in our lifetime. As the earth's surface warms over the next decade, ocean temperatures will undoubtedly follow at a slower pace, and ultimately affect the Tomales Bay and its oyster industry.

139

Acknowledgements

This project started out as something small. It grew into a book with a lot of encouragement, patience and support from Chris Gruener at Cameron + Company and Doreen Schmid, writer and editor. My heartfelt thanks to them. Many others contributed to this book and I greatly appreciate their willingness to be part of it.

Appreciation to Charles Friend of Tomales Bay Oyster Company for his instigation of the idea way back in 2003, and for generously providing access to his farm, his knowledge and information, support and many, many bags of oysters. To Francis Boudreau for so eloquently describing how to eat an oyster on page 84. To Luc Chamberland for his wine notes and passion for everything to do with oysters, and to his family for taking me on some of my first boat rides on the Bay. To Matisse Manual for his boots in the cover photograph.

To Shannon Gregory, Tyler Fitts and Kim Laboa at The Marshall Store and Heidi Gregory at TBOC for their encouragement of and enthusiasm for the project. Eloise Christensen of the natural space for her typographic direction, Stacy Lauer for styling The Marshall Store recipes. Michelle Dotter for copy editing, and Brett Poirer, Leslie Adler Ivanbrook, and Melinda Leithold.

To everyone who generously gave of their time and information, including Chris Starbird; Terry Sawyer of Hog Island and Ginny, Nancy and Bridgit Lunny of Drakes Bay Oyster Farm. To NPS archivist Carola de Rooy for her time and interest, Susan Hall for her perspective on Hamlet, and *The Point Reyes Light* for their archives.

For their recipes:
Hog Island Oyster Company: p91
Aluxa Lalicker of The Oyster Girls: p92, 109
Janis Laboa of The Marshall Store: p103
Shannon Gregory of The Marshall Store: p103, 106, 109, 110, 113, 114
Kim Laboa of Indian Peach Catering Company: p117
Christian Caiazzo of Osteria Stellina: p118, 122
Adam Mali at Nicks Cove: p121, 124
Nancy Lunny at Drakes Bay Oyster Company: p126
Wayne Pratt at The Station House: p129, 130

Bibliography

Avery, Christy. "Tomales Bay Environmental History and Historic Resource Study, Pacific West Region." National Park Service, U.S. Department of the Interior: 2009.

Babalis, Timothy. "A Historical Perspective on the National Research Council's Report Shellfish Mariculture in Drakes Estero.'" National Park Service, U.S. Department of the Interior: 2009.

Baker, Anne. "Park Service to demolish old Jensen's oyster farm." *Point Reyes Light,* November 7, 1996.

Bancroft, Hubert Howe. *Chronicles of the Builders of the Commonwealth,* Volume 4: San Francisco: The History Company, 1891.

Barrett, Elinore M. "The California Oyster industry." *The Resource Agency of California Department of Fish and Game Fish Bulletin 123*: 1963 (issued) http://content.cdlib.org.

Bartley, Devin and Moore. "Status of the fisheries report, an update through 2008." California Department of Fish and Game Marine Region: August 2010.

Bradley, Larken. "Jensen's oyster beds—a life of hard work." *Point Reyes Light*, March 23, 2000.

Bush, Lisa. "The Marin Coastal Watershed Enhancement Project." University of California Cooperative Extension, Novato: November 1995.

Carson, Rob. "Water Quality in the bay and watershed: What we have learned from monitoring." Presentation, State of the Bay Conference, Tomales Bay Watershed Council, Inverness: October 2010.

Chesapeake Bay Program, "Oyster Management and Restoration." December 8, 2009 <http://www.chesapeakebay.net>.

County of Marin, Department of Agricultural Weights and Measures, "Marin County Crop Report, 1939—2009." County of Marin: 1939—2009 <http://www.co.marin.ca.us>.

Conte, Fred S. "California Aquaculture." University of California at Davis, Department of Animal Science: February 1996.

Duthie, Jo et al. "Historic Study." Marin County Local Coastal Program. Marin County Planning Department: November 1981.

Dell, Shari-Faye. "Tomales Bay Oyster Company." *West Marin Citizen*: July 2, 2009. Dumas, Alexandre. Colman, Louis, ed. Dictionary of Cuisine. New York: Avon Books, 1958.

Egan, Gloria. "It's Unanimous; Plan is Repealed." *Point Reyes Light*, August 12, 1971.

Ehat, Carla and Kent, Anne. Interview with Arthur Giddings, Oral Histories Marin County, October 11, 1977 <http://www.co.marin.ca.us>.

Filion, Ron S. "Succulent Bivalves From the Atlantic Coast Thrive in Local Beds." *San Francisco Call*, April 20, 1909 <http://www.sfgenealogy.com>.

Gahagan, Mike. "To the Point, Maybe we'd be a railroad town again." *Point Reyes Light*, October 28, 1971.

Largier, John, Dr. "Tomales Bay Oceanography and how Climate Change may Alter Bay Environments." Presentation, State of the Bay Conference, Tomales Bay Watershed Council, Inverness: October 2010.

Livingston, Dewey. "Hamlet 1844-1988, A History of Jensen's Oyster Beds." *Historic Resource Study, Point Reyes National Seashore.* Point Reyes National Park Service,1989.

Marin County Free Library. "Riding the Railroad in Marin County, circa 1900." Anne T. Kent California Room, San Rafael, California.

Mason, Jack. "Charlie's Oysters." *Point Reyes Historian,* 1980.

Mason, Jack. *Summer Town, The History of Inverness, California.* North Shore Books: Inverness, 1974.

Monterey Bay Aquarium. "Turning the Tide: The State of Seafood." Monterey Bay Aquarium, Monterey, CA: 2009.

National Park Service Conservation Study Institute. "Stewardship Begins with People: an Atlas of Places, People and Handmade Products." National Park Service: Vermont, 2007.

National Park Service. "Giacomini Wetlands Restoration: A Legacy for Tomales Bay." U.S. Department of the Interior: September 2010.

Nevin, George. "Truce Reached in Tomales Bay Herring War." *Marin Independent Journal,* December 4, 1976.

Philpots, John Richards. *Oysters and All About Them.* London: Richardson & Co., 1890.

Rheault, Robert B. "Ecosystem Services Provided by Shellfish Aquaculture." February 2010 <http://longislandsoundstudy.net>.

Rheault, Robert B. "Oyster Culture is Good for the Environment." Date unknown <http://www.coonamessettfarm.com>.

Rilla, Ellie and Bush, Lisa. "The Changing Role of Agriculture in Point Reyes National Seashore." University of California Cooperative Extension, Novato: 2009 < http://cemarin.ucdavis.edu>.

Russell, Ann, Dr. "Impacts of Ocean Acidification and Climate Change on Estuarine and Coastal Organisms." Presentation, State of the Bay Conference, Tomales Bay Watershed Council, Inverness: October 2010.

Sculati, Christine. "Still Hanging On: The Bay's Native Oysters." *Bay Nature*: December 2004.

Shafer, Chris A. "The Public Trust Doctrine and Wetlands Protection: Modern Application of an Ancient Doctrine." Presentation, International Symposium, Wetlands, Michigan: 2006.

Stevens, Jan S. "Protecting California's Rivers: Confluence of Science, Policy and Law Applying the Public Trust Doctrine to River Protection."University of California at Davis: June 9, 2004.

Stratton, Patsy. "Virginia Jensen & daughters do it all in busy Tomales Bay oyster operation." *Empire Farmer*, March 1978.

Surface Water Ambient Monitoring Program (SWAMP). "The status of perennial estuarine wetlands in the state of California." SWAMP, Sacramento: December 2010.

Toba, Derrick. "Small-scale Oyster Farming for Pleasure and Profit in Washington." Washington Sea Grant Publications Office, Seattle: 2002.